*for my dad*

This is how one pictures the angel of history. His face is turned toward the past. Where we perceive a chain of events, he sees one single catastrophe which keeps piling wreckage upon wreckage and hurls it in front of his feet. The angel would like to stay ... But a storm is blowing from Paradise; it has got caught in his wings with such violence that the angel can no longer close them. The storm irresistibly propels him into the future to which his back is turned, while the pile of debris before him grows skyward.

Walter Benjamin


Then I will headlong run into the earth

Marlowe, *Faustus*

# Contents

## RESURRECTION FAIL

I've heard people say
that when we die
we will surely have
a heart-to-heart
with Christ.
Wouldn't that be nice?
I'd ask him,
Why let my grandpa,
when his mind
scattered in the winds,
wander the Bronx
in his pajamas that day,
he who like a cat
was most afraid
of indignity?
I'd ask,
Is it a *joke* to yoke us
one to another
with love
just to yank us apart,
like parodies of the sacred?

I'd definitely ask
about Muhammad Niaz.
Christ might try
to interject
but I'll be on a roll.
You probably recall,
Christ, I'd say,
that "mystic" in Pakistan
named Sabir,
bored by the same
old miracles,
who told the crowd

in a little square
he could reanimate the dead.
All he needed
was a volunteer,
someone who'd like
to experience the afterlife
*and come back.*
Niaz stepped out.
Niaz was perfect:
forty, day laborer,
wife, six kids.
He didn't want to leave
this world, at all.
He *believed.*
Sabir led Niaz to a table,
tied his hands
and legs with rope,
and cut his throat.

Christ might say,
Is that a question?
Christ, the corpse of Niaz
is your corpse.
We the children
of Niaz
no longer want you
to come back.
We have made a heaven of corpses
here on earth.
Hands clasped in reverence
for what we see.
Soaked
in the rain of it.

## THE EPIC OF SENGE

We brought our big old tomcat
from India to Philadelphia.
Tried to keep him in our row house
but he longed for village life:
fighting cats, hunting rats, walking the roofs
of the huts. He cried his lungs out.
Sleepless, defeated, we opened the door:
Senge padded out in triumph.
He walked the sidewalks of West Philly,
manifesting all the lavish beauty
and violence of the village.
Every day he got lost.

Today Tiina and I comb
the misty late-summer streets, searching.
Tiina, whose love for that cat
is fugitive and powerful,
is so worried she can't talk.

We step into Clark Park. I joke,
"Maybe he caught a boat
back to India?" Tiina emits a small,
dry laugh. We scan the park.
Dogs: fourteen. Cats: zero.
But it's nice. We sit in the damp grass.
Someone in a pandemic mask
strums a woozy guitar. Soft,
distant singing. The sky, opening.

Under a maple tree: a pile, a form,
it is a body, a possum. Twisted, seeping,
torn like a bag of rice. I say nothing.

Everything is wet. Record rain this year.
Even the kindness hovering in the high branches
is wet, glittering, pretty. Almost unbearable.
And familiar. The peaceful men
playing chess on metal tables.
The children blowing bubbles of light.

Like attending a warmhearted funeral
which just happens to be your own.

## SUPERSPREADER

So many diseases swirling in the air around our heads
like tiny wasps with goblin claws!
Is the invisible world as horrifying as they say?
Best not to fret, to overthink the
swarming maladies uncountable around you
right now, this second, some flying up your nose,
some clattering past like rag and bone men
with shopping carts under a Kensington bridge,
or hungry prophets in a field of lightning.
From what I understand, your paranoia is apt.
Who wouldn't be terrified of a ninja-like nemesis
creeping into the village while you sleep,
troubadours in torn waistcoats unpacking
weird barbed instruments, playing quiet music
that makes you erupt in pustules and buboes,
or cough blood, suddenly your immune system
crashes, bone marrow fizzing with useless antibodies
(which, I learned on *House M.D.*, is called amyloidosis)?
Grandma warned my mom, don't put your arm
on the armrest at movies or pushers will jab you
with dope. Best not dwell on that. Best forget
all the infections and germs spiraling like satellites
or pirates. To live in peace we need quietness,
worry-free-ness, eating a slice of pizza in the sun.
Put out of your mind the fact that you could at any second
be grazed by a virus—even Napoleon, *L'Ogre de Corse*,
flinched when touched by a plague victim
of Jaffa, in the painting by Antoine-Jean Gros—
or be coughed on by some tubercular *other*,
carrier, spreader, superspreader, or be standing too near
Chernobyl-level radiation, precipitating diarrhea,
headaches, seizures, loss of muscle function

and, soon enough, a rectangular wooden coat,
then heaven's gate. We're so damn delicate—
the wind sweeping through us—like Aeolian harps.

# At the Barnes Museum on a Cold Fall Afternoon

*for Matthew Wong, 1984-2019*

Over my quinoa salad I admit
to the old couple from Chattanooga
who have come all this way to see the Van Goghs
that I think Van Gogh is corny
or maybe just reproduced too often
in lacquered frames in waiting rooms
of dentists. The kind of day
strangers keep chatting to me
and I keep putting my foot in my mouth.

This morning my mother said
I should go to the Barnes, on her and Dad,
to help me find closure with M.
Her words. So here I sit
in the café, sipping coffee beside
the old couple from Chattanooga,
under a big window, blue sky.
I've got that almond-stuck-in-
my-throat feeling, which means
I should cry but haven't. The husband
nods at me, chews, stares. The wife,
Bonnie, says, Oh yes she supposes
Van Gogh is corny, but don't I think
his lines hold the earth together?
Now I stand eye to eye, as Bonnie
said I should, with Van Gogh's *Postman*,
trying not to picture the 37-year-old painter
rolled up in a ball, bullet in his gut,
alone in his room at the Auberge Ravoux inn.

In August, 2015, M. texted me a poem
of his called "Vincent": "All around
The shirts of children are laughing
And chasing each other's tails.
I smile." Above the postman's beard
and his fuck-you eyebrows and *Postes* hat,
Vincent scrawled "Vincent" in
red childlike cursive on the green
wallpaper of swirling flowers,
flowers chasing each other's tails,
like the flowers in M.'s paintings, ever-
blossoming. And, yes, Bonnie is right,
holding everything together,
even me and M., and now I'm crying
so even the tour group can see,
but that does not stop Nikki,
ironic mermaid clip in her green hair,
from asking if I've heard of
this German kid, Mikail Akar,
who's a better painter than Picasso,
wilder, feral-er, more singular
than Picasso, she says, while standing
beside *L'Ascète*, that joyless skinny
blue guy with his sad lump of bread,
painted by 22-year-old Picasso
seventy years before his heart gave out
while he ate with his wife and friends.
In the last year of M.'s life,
before he stepped away from us,
before he erased himself
and his stammering affection
for his friends, and his inspiration,
before he erased his long arms
and dour face to immerse himself

in nullity, he and I hadn't talked much,
which is why I can't explain
his specific grief to you.

I'm gazing up at Matisse's dancers,
his summer of all dancers,
Matisse who died of a heart attack
at eighty-four, beside Lydia
Délectorskaya, his model
and friend of twenty years, who
when she was sure he was dead
picked up the suitcase
she'd kept packed the whole time
and walked out the door.
Grief sticks to me, every burr of grief
I've brushed against, the grief
I've drawn a kind of circle around today,
as suggested by my generous mother,
this circle of paintings that we,
accidentally united, gather inside,
almonds in our throats, burrs on our skin
from all that's clawed and
scratched us since our births.

M. would not like this poem.
It's too long, already. And soft.
But, about that, M., what surprised me
was not your quicksilver talent,
your sudden fame, your solo shows
in Paris, New York, Hong Kong,
but the sweetness of your paintings:
the sentiment, the glitter, the flowers.
So many small figures clasping their hearts,
overcome with inward feeling.

Strange, all this, coming from one
who never found a way to enjoy,
as Kafka described it, the happiness
of being with people. You'd
embarrass us, saying, Wow, you look
terrible today, didn't you sleep?
Talking about yourself so unrelentingly
I had to yawn and turn away.

In a room of Modiglianis
a fella with cat whiskers
shakes my hand, his name is Ronald,
he taps the motorcycle patch
on my jacket, Be careful will ya,
Ronald says, still shaking my hand,
squeezing it, My son died on a bike.
There's a Polaroid of M.
as a kid, I saw it on CBC News,
with a look on his face, haggard,
plagued, raging, like an old man.
Now, my gifted friend, my quirky friend,
you are dead. And this poem
which you'd have thought absurd
is for you. Or would you, maybe, I hope,
with your secret sentimentality,
have been flattered? Did you know
Modigliani was thirty-five
when he died? Like you. But unlike you,
who were alone, he—drenched
in sweat, delirious, in the throes of TB
—held his pregnant girlfriend,
Hébuterne, in bed. A man
in a stovepipe hat hums to himself
and sunset falls over the walls

of paintings around me.
I shut my eyes against a Modigliani.
But I still see it, you know it,
that defiant boy in a sailor's suit,
hands on his knees,
mouth opened in a sneer.

# Dog Songs

Child actor Jackie Cooper
loved dogs. In 1931,
on the set of the comedy *Skippy,*
Director Norman Taurog
to help Cooper act sad
threatened to kill the boy's dog.
It worked! Cooper cried
and vomited till he was sedated.

I tried to find the name
of that dog but
could not. That story
is about the star.
The dog illustrates
Jackie Cooper's ability
to love.

Would Cooper
if not dead of old age
be repulsed by the stray dogs
here in Gamru, India?
I wish he could see
these two three-legged dogs
play in the road!
I think he'd enjoy them
despite their bony ribs
and seeping wounds.

When Buddha said
"I don't quarrel with the world,
the world quarrels with me,"
I think he meant

that feeling of trying to sleep
while local dogs
bark their fool heads off
outside your window.

On holiday in Odisha,
Tiina and I were delighted
to meet the red dogs
of Puri. "Why," I asked
one romantic evening
walking the shore
holding hands at dusk,
"are they *all* red?"

The Chinantecs of Oaxaca
believe when you die
a dog helps you cross the water
to the land of the dead.

"I don't know," Tiina said
as puppy after puppy
washed up beside us
on the surf.

# 2016

The night Carlos leaves
for Brazil, his home,
six of us sit with him
on our terrace in Gamru
under a single bulb.
Wet stone tiles, a cat,
a dog, a tall sunflower.
Édith Piaf moans on tinny speakers.

The constant monsoon rains
just stopped, seconds ago.
Air clear and cool
with a taste of smoke
from burning garbage.
Far-off porchlights on the hills
blink and a distant taxi
screams like a hurt monkey.

Piaf's voice an urgent siren:
*"Nonnnn, Je Ne Regrette Riennnnn ..."*
"A lovely song," Carlos says.
He wears a salmon polo shirt,
a mala around his wrist,
flowering lotus tattoo on his neck.
It's hard to know if he's weak
or just still. And *skinny*, too skinny,
jaw too big in his head.
He's had HIV eight years.

"But," he says, "what's *wrong*
with regret?" I jump in:
"Of course we should let go

of regret. Why hold onto bitterness?"
We are all quiet. Tiina pours tea,
one eye on Carlos.
He says, gently, warmly,
not to embarrass me,
"Like that night I wasn't careful."

The lightest sound, wingbeats.
A million moths creeping
the wall beside us, wings stamped
with antiquated signs—
mandalas, dragons, goblets, crucifixes—
a living mosaic shattering, slow.
A soul crawling out of itself.
Crawling out and out and out of itself.

# I Received a Bitter Email from a Good-Hearted Man

So twenty years of friendship
ended in a small gesture
like a door sliding shut,
and I carried my feeling
to the roof, with its clear view
of Gamru, villagers strolling by,
men with their cigarettes,
women with bags of sand
on their heads, a few thin dogs.
It was a sick, empty feeling,
like a film of ash on the skin.
And general, too, the feeling
—in the air, in the spectral smoke.
Not for me alone. I circled
the roof, but slowly, slowly,
like Issa's snail. I spoke aloud
to the green parrots in a tree
about my friend. I told them
how he let me sleep on his couch
so many nights, and read me
his poems until the wee hours,
poems that made me feel
like part of a tribe. I told them
I hoped he'd be all right,
more than all right, without my help,
which he'd always had till now.
A butterfly cut a jagged line
in the air and I said to the parrots
that for me this is enough,
all of this. And as I spoke it
I believed it. I inhaled, in a deep breath,
the farm and wide roof and the sky

and almost threw up, the melancholy
so sharp. How blessed I was,
it didn't seem real, like a gardener
who keeps finding seeds
in the creases of his clothes,
and pressed against his skin.
As if I knew, more than any god,
how to live. Suddenly the parrots
darted to the opposite hill,
making a green ladder in the air,
leaving behind a sweet afterimage
which I shut my eyes
to see a moment longer.

## A Big Black Wave

I receive an anthology in the mail
and open to a poem by David
Hernandez. "I don't hunt," he says,
"but wish every deer wore a bulletproof vest."
I like it. He's obsessed, he explains
in a note, with Elizabeth Bishop's
"In the Waiting Room." I find it
online. Bishop describes herself as a kid
peering at adults in a dentist's office,
reading *National Geographic*, overwhelmed
by the multitude and variety of bodies
in the world; suddenly the room
"was sliding / beneath a big black wave."
I watch a schoolgirl on YouTube
recite it, fast, unburdened by sense.
I click on a video of giraffes fighting
to comical ragtime piano music.
They bat each other with their faces!
Swinging neck and head like a bag
with a brick in it. Who conceived
such an animal, made of puzzle pieces?
A child god? Even in violence
they are fragile. As if it hurt them to hurt.
I click on a video of a giraffe being shot
to death. I watch it five times.
A male like a lighthouse in the desert
staggers on stick legs. Blood
spurts below his neck, at the collar.
A thread breaks and he falls back
on himself. The ground rises to meet him.
His neck unrolls like parchment,
like a river. His massive body shudders,

grasping for what is indestructible.
Druidical knobs of his head in sand.
His wound retches. Two vultures
stroll into the frame, unhurried,
feathered bankers. One pokes its beak
deep in the eye of the living giraffe,
like a key.

## 2014

Packing for India, a photo of Inge surfaced:
college graduation, black turtleneck,
hair across the eyes. Pretty.
A rare inward moment I still love.

She holds a schedule, parents nearby (always
them), in her blue robes and flat hat,
waist-deep in the black water of dusk.
No way I'd recall any of this
without the photo. I slip it in the pile,

too late. We danced to ABBA's
*"Voulez-Vous."* We crawled,
in our first ecstasy, burgundy carpets.
Why the nostalgia, suddenly,
in middle age? Pain, *ex post facto?*

I open my laptop to the internet's
nether regions, a couple in underwear
on a webcam, grainy sepia, bored,
waiting to *do it* if somebody pays.
She on her stomach, facing us,
topless, one foot in the air,
one foot on the man behind her:
on his back across the bed,
black Speedo, head cut off
by the frame on the right.
Camera cockeyed, as in a film
by Godard, outtake of *Breathless*.

The lamp and bedframe, dumpy.
Are they saving for another place?
Has he deceived her? The man,
pulling hard on his cigarette (smoke
hovers), peers up—I *know* he peers up
—at dusk through the skylight,
at a bird, a seabird, white, an albatross
floating in figure eights.

## RAIS BHUIYAN SONG

*A man who embarked on a shooting spree in what he*
*claimed was retaliation for 9/11 has been executed at*
*a prison in Texas. The lone survivor of Mark Stroman's*
*attack on convenience store workers in late 2001, Rais*
*Bhuiyan, originally from Bangladesh, unsuccessfully*
*sued to stop the execution ...*
            —The Guardian, July 21, 2011

Rais Bhuiyan, what is mercy?
You tried to stop
the state from killing
the racist meth head
who shot you *in the face*,
while I'm still mad
at women who left ages ago,
at friends who don't call,
even at John H.
who killed himself last year.
Why, Rais Bhuiyan, did he *do* that,
and why am I rattled
by things that have
so little to do with me?
Can mercy release me
from the dread that grew
out of that grade six
"trust game," when the kids,
*my friends*, let me fall
between their fingers?
Don't you, like me, stumble
through such brambles
and barbs each night, bloodied,
into the woods of sleep?

I tried to worship the streets
of Tai Po, Hong Kong—
where Tiina and I lived
when I found your story
—the mahjong tables, the towers, the lovers,
then after ten minutes
of limping feral cats
and cruel fathers
I caught myself scratching curses
on a public toilet, like Raskolnikov.
Rais Bhuiyan, I'm bad
at mercy. Is it like sitting
in the back of a taxi
and the driver's in a great mood,
singing in Cantonese,
catching every light?
My heart is like my favorite
old shirt: filthier each day
and will not get clean.
Is mercy a gate you squeeze past
by smearing your body
in shit? Is mercy an amnesiac?
Ill will o'erflows the tub.
Surely an opposite faction
gathers in a forest,
ones like you
performing the maenad's
empathetic dance,
a lay-down-your-guns dance
for the rest of us.
Rais Bhuiyan, shall I just repeat
the irrational list of kindnesses
my mother used to speak
while touching my small back,

till the ill-will-shaped animals bow
in the fields of birth—
just as Mark Stroman,
he who shotgunned you,
bowed his head
after his lethal injection?

# HOW TO FLOAT

My mother writes me details of
her holiday in Goa. *A man is snoring
in the next hut. A big rock in the sea
is covered with crabs.* I can just see her
at an internet cafe typing emails,
air thick with incense and Germans
smeared with coconut sunscreen.

People used to ask if we were sister
and brother. No more. She's
frailer, child-like. Nervous.
Mothers are strange. Primal force
ramming against the ego.
How do they find peace?
She writes, *I just sink to the bottom!*

*How do you float?* She's so thin.
Does she have the body fat?
Was she buoyant before *me*?
Before my father? What invisible
anvil does she hold? Any little thing
can wreck you. Maybe her dad
winced at a drawing of hers. Perhaps,

in the water, we must become
someone lighter. A lady who skips work
to smoke clove cigars and play
the marimba. I mean, why don't we
drown every time we see a photo
of an elephant, face hacked off
by poachers? I picture my mother

wading to the dark edge of the sand
where fear begins. She *should* float.
Look at her. Porous as balsa.
Guileless as an apple. I write her,
"Just fill your lungs, have fun!"
I wish I'd said, "Please avoid
the ocean! It's fucking terrifying."

## Resurrection Fail

"The Moon over Auschwitz"
was the original title
of this poem. I stared at it
so long I lost track
of what that moon
shone upon. I thought,
I can't write that,
I'm not Jewish,
I've never even been
to Poland. I did not mean
harm. Moon
can mean sorrow:
as in, I read how the dark
side of the moon
is actually turquoise
which glows like ice
over the barracks
of Birkenau. Now
you are googling me
to confirm that I am,
as you guessed,
a white dude. You doubt
that bad things
have happened to me.
I doubt it, too. So many
bad poems are litanies of
personal trauma
peppered with trope,
one would think
stepping into daylight is enough
to horrify us all,
but isn't it? How different

is the Auschwitz moon
from the moon over
Philadelphia? Each drifts over us
like a clod washed away
by the sea. I did walk
the Villa Medici in moonglow
between goddess statues
which like clouds have no face.
Or is that *La Dolce Vita*,
or *The Tale of Zatoichi?*
Yes it's the blind swordsman
Zatoichi touching the lovely face
of the sister of a yakuza.
They are falling in love.
Zatoichi's fingers
in the language of movies
are aspects of the moon.
Have you ever seen the moon
on a sunny afternoon
out of nowhere?
Like a watermark in the desert,
like a thin man
I washed dishes with
who kept taking breaks
to read Phillis Wheatley.
When you're drowsy
or stoned, when you're really
not looking—
then the moon comes,
its kidskin grin,
the Padre Pio cuts
in each of its palms,
while far below
down here

fire rises upwards
water flows downwards
love spirals
outwards
and hour after hour
we carry our dead out of its light
like ants.

# Uncle Mike at a KFC in Yonkers

Dad's old friend, my godfather
stares hard
at his fried chicken biscuit,
slurring how great it is to see me
after twenty-six years.
The Uncle Mike I remember
was skinny, elfin,
card tricks, dirty jokes,
winking. He bought me
shiny new shoes,
tossing my old shoes
out the window of his Studebaker!

The ventilation fans
above our booth chop
and clank against
the great heat of the earth.

Six years ago, Uncle Mike
caught a thief stealing his car.
The man, instead of running,
cracked Uncle Mike's skull
with a gun. Infection
swept his brain like brush fire.
Parkinson's. In two years
he'll be in the ground.

Uncle Mike is recounting, laboriously,
a recent news story
about Umar Farouk
Abdulmutallab, the Nigerian
who tried to blow up

a jet to Detroit, strapping
chemicals to his leg,
stepping out of the toilet
eyes flaming
like the Lord of Death himself, only to be
ignobly seized.

A cop shovels gravied taters
under a breathtaking moustache,
nodding as if hearing
distantly
the sound of bluegrass.
*Eyes flaming*, Uncle Mike repeats.
He raises
observing some private ritual
a fried breast to his lips.
*I shoulda never*, he slurs,
fingers shaking badly,
*tried to stop that stupid fuck.*

## MORNING AFTER A PARTY IN A FARMHOUSE

I lie on a hard bed
scanning my body
for a joy I can use like pliers
to pry my way
into the morning.
Downstairs my friends
gobble pancakes
in a hangover frenzy.

Last night
I sat with a dear friend
on a firewood pile
as she described
the fingers of her
childhood piano teacher,
how as he played
with his left hand deftly
his right dragged
down her thigh,
up her school skirt
and down again,
up and down
like waves on a shore.
Listening to her
I had on a silly orange wig
I couldn't figure out
how to take off.

The house tomcat jumps up
to sit on my chest,
looking at the wheat field
through the window

like King David
gazing at Jerusalem.
Each morning
he returns from the brook
smeared in blood,
in his mouth
one of night's creatures
demystified.

My dream ignites
like a flare in the dark.
I'd been naked,
holding my sword
in a forest,
no enemy in sight.
Like one of the dead
catapulted
out of the earth.
Nothing happened.
I just stood there,
breathing.
Effect of a missing cause.
So the light I gave off
was my own.

# The Handsomest Man in the Neighborhood

As you walked by
Alex waved his hammer
big smile
descending a ladder
from the blind windows
of his house
its constant renovations
Alex stood before you
in your path
even if your grocery bags
cut your palms
but he had such a sweet look
and spoke with such
forthrightness about his life
it was hard to be mad

His wife Anu
she was Norwegian
she was well
he had just been canoeing
with his family
that went well
he loved his job
youth coordinator for Katimavik
at times he went on so long
you tried to fracture it all
saying
Don't you think time
will be overtaken by weather?

This made his pupils
go black as cart grease
but then he'd surprise you

sharing details
so personal
you could not hate him
for his preppy shirts
with the collars up
he'd tell you his young daughter
who made him
want to hook his thumbs
on his tool belt
collected crickets
in a bear-shaped honey bottle
then released them
in the backyard
and months later

I heard it was her
the daughter
who discovered Alex's body
in their hall
hanging there
a moth its wings tucked in
I never met his daughter
but I picture
the frazzled lady
at the grocery store
gesturing to the cereal boxes
shouting
*These ones here they are*
then gibberish
like a bright lamp
flickering
throwing shadows
all around it

# WHEN I HEARD MY CHILDHOOD NAME CRIED OUT

Even before the fire
That summer afternoon
Our cottage in Nova Scotia
Seemed to be melting
Like a sugar cube
In the mouth of a donkey
The field above it
A shade of violet
My father heaping sticks
And shrubs in a pile and when he lit it
The fire marched
Up the field ragged spitting rude
A motley army
Humming a merry song
Wind the song
The field a feather
Barb aflame
Meantime inside I lay on my back
On hardwood
A book I loved above me
*O and the sea the sea*
*crimson sometimes like fire and*
*the glorious sunsets*
*and the figtrees in*
*the Alameda gardens yes*
When I heard my childhood name
Cried out
It was my mother
Dad laughing
I stepped outside
My mother keeping pace solemnly
With tufts of blue

Incandescent elementals

Fire

It's okay it's okay Dad was saying don't worry guys

As flame sipped the trees

Like a bear a waterfall

Then came a caravan of trucks

Local housefathers

Uncombed dignitaries in high boots

Astronauts upon the green

Men who know damn well

What side of the bread to butter

My mother waved

Dad spoke to each

And the men unamused stamped

Upon the light

Crushing in a dance the afterfeather

As Dad walked the blistering ruts

Their trucks had made

Strolled into the cottage

Slid on a Thelonious Monk record

Put his feet up

Lit a cigar

# SWIMMING IN CHURCH LAKE, NOVA SCOTIA

That thundercloud, north, is a bathtub
overflowing silver.
The man with the beard
is my father. What current
urges me to the road,
him to the forest?
My mother hugs her knees
on the big granite stone.
I am the son with tinnitus
from rock concerts.
A quiet dentist drill
just over my skull
shifting one ear to the other.
Below us, lake bottom,
a black cloud flowers.
The feather of dusk upon us.
Light, a dragonfly, scatters.
Waterskaters.
The man with the beard
swims out further.
We are a triangle of waves.
I am the rattlebrained
son. That sound is the
mind treading water.
I am the bearded man.
I keep the colorblind distances.
I am the woman.
The trembling celestial
ladder my body.
I am love,
keeping the triangle large.
I am thunder
my ear sings.

# A LOST CAUSE

My remedies for you, my love, *suck*.
You just perish and perish.
You perished giggling like a goat
when you heard Charles II,
with his revolting overbite,
took the throne. You let yourself
be murdered by that nimrod Nimrod.
Even now you twist out of my arms
into the reviled gray yonder
like a ruined yogi. Too frail. Diaphanous
as curtains. Perishing by the 1000's
at Troy. Bitten, cooking snake soup,
by a cobra's severed head. It is
your ludicrous talent. I turn away
half a second, you drive into a wall.
You hemorrhage, you fall. Famine,
epidemic, natural marvel. Force majeure,
Molotov cocktail. We toss you
into a mass grave. What did you expect?
How, my love, can I even grieve?
You perish again as I hold this pen.
Needless to say, you're no Charlemagne,
clawing your way back to resume
the crusade. And how stupid you are.
After fourteen plates of your favorite dessert
(a sweet roll in a bowl of hot milk,
called *hetvägg*) you perish of indigestion.
I admit, you do it well. But is it *all*
you can do? Storm-chaser, friend,
all I've been doing, all I can do,
as the planet staggers and crumbles
beneath us, is hold you.

## POLYAMORY SONG

At thirty, divorced, feeling geriatric,
I dated Natalie: very pretty, fun,
              nineteen. I, not handsome,

felt lucky. We had polyamorous friends
so Nat and I gave it a try. Bad idea.
              She could smoke a joint, fall into bed

with a woman or man, never think of it again.
I wanted that. To be as chill as Leonard Cohen
              who didn't want to talk of love or chains

and things we can't untie. But chains
braced me. And I liked Nat.
              I slept around, yes, but

imagining Nat naked with another
twisted me. She'd gladly spill
              every detail. I listened,

trying to be cool—my eyes
subzero spotlights on her face.
              Nervous and still as a squirrel.

Later, alone, I lay in bed. Angst
flew in the window, circling,
              flapping its wings.

Picturing Nat with some faceless
jackhammer of a dude, I pulled the blanket over me.
              I can do polygamy, I thought,

almost weeping. People do it!
I'll just figure it out, like a trick pilot,
                like that pilot who landed a plane

       on St. Nicholas Ave, Manhattan, 1956—
with no lights, no radio,
              finding a way through

       the maze of buildings, crisscrossing wires,
bystanders, to glide down to earth
              without harming anyone.

# SONG FOR JUST BEFORE DISASTER

We don't say often enough
how sweet it is before the ruin.

That's why *The Godfather* begins
with a wedding, a *nice* wedding,
before Brando gets shot. It was good,

really good, before it fell apart.
We know the change is coming
and that it will hurt. But still

we fantasize it isn't and it won't.

The terrifying beauty of Quauhnahuac,
in *Under the Volcano*, is only possible
if the Consul dies in the morning.

So each page, as the Ferris wheel
turns, is this long held breath
before. Like a party where you're
having a beautiful conversation,

which you relish because you know
eventually the police will come,
the lights will get flipped on.
It felt that way the night before

Tiina and I left India. I went up
to the roof to see the mountains
against the purple stormclouds
and smell the village smoke.
Someone was singing in one of the huts.

Ever watch a ball of paper burn,
up close? It flickers, folds,
collapses on itself like a house.
Sublime for an instant,
then ash. Or twenty-two years ago,

the month with Dominique
before we fought, before I
annoyed her. When I was steady
and she treated me softly.
Then it was my recent divorce

I refused to feel, like the boy
with his thumb in the dike:
my compulsions and neediness
close and building hideously.

But for that one month, *ah*,
Dominique's roommate was away,
it was just us two, she'd made
a living space in the basement:

a bed by the furnace, soft lamplight,
French CDs, Georges Brassens'
*"Le Gorille"* on repeat. That basement
held a strange melancholy force,

not despite but because us together
was an awful idea. That feeling—
enjoy yourself, this is going to sting.
All right, no contest. Reap
what's sown later. Over and over

we fucked, me giving myself
desperately, her on top, my finger
in her asshole, her moaning my name.

## RESURRECTION FAIL

At a street vendor in Hong Kong
in the smoke of chestnuts
came a vision:
the very last time with Inge
my erection a wound in the air
in our tiny flat in Rome.

Not having touched in months
What are you doing, touching yourself?
she asked. Maybe, I said. Well
all right, she said.
I kneeled between her legs
and she who once saw a gentleness in me
raised herself to my hips
so I saw her again
with all her faces at once
like a village,
the villagers walking out
to the night forest
bearing the beloved in their arms
the one who would die
that night.

They circled the beloved
singing the oldest songs
with full hearts
and when at last
those eyes fluttered shut, the sun
came bearing
the slightest warmth.

# It Was Our Honeymoon after All

We drove down the coast
sun roof open
singing Tom Waits
top of our lungs.
Inge's one eye shut
when she sang.
We made Oregon by dusk.
She'd booked us
a place on the ocean.
We bust in like kids.
Look at the bamboo lamp!
Look at the ocean!

I wrote a poem. The ice machine
was in the poem,
stamping its foot
like a flamenco dancer.
Inge, those years,
was in every poem.
I described her
in a white hotel robe,
framed by the bathroom door,
hair dripping,
toweling her hair,
head cocked
at me. I opened a window,
turned off the lamp.
It was dark,
she let the robe slip.

We divorced
and don't talk. The poem
lost. A day buried
in the earth of days.
But the sun bled
like a prison tattoo.
Where parking lot
met beach,
God stood on a trash pile
squawking nonsense.

## I Saw Two Beat Poets at an Elks Club with a Girl in My English Class

We stood at the back, her smoking,
spiked blonde hair, biker jacket,
                    much cooler than me.

I sipped beer, nervous, chattering
about "that Ginsberg sound"
                    —when out *he* stepped,

big granny glasses, grey prophet's
beard, pumping a harmonium,
                    chanting:

> *Bush paid Noriega, used to work together*
> *They sat on a couch*
> *& talked about the weather ...*

Who was this tuneless
dorky grandpa? Where was the goblin sea hag
                    that once sang

out of that mouth?
I stared, heartsick. Gregory Corso
                    swaggered out,

head of hair, horn-rimmed specs,
black blazer. Edgier, tighter,
                    *better*. My date nodded hiply

till Corso tripped, cockeyed
drunk. Spell broken.
                    I stopped reading them;

never saw my classmate
out of class again. Now, thirty-one years later,
                    I'm the age,

        almost, of those old swans,
who weren't so bad, really,
                    just bone-tired.

        Comes a tap at the window,
a figure, I *know* them,
                    the Chernobyl eyes,

        the duende fingernails. I step out
into humid West Philly. They
                    are bald, quick, shoeless,

        in sackcloth and ashes.
We walk, they talk, a non-
                    stop rhizomatic whine,

        reckoning for me
which strangers play piano by ear,
                    which conceal handguns

        under their coats;
who was knifed here,
                    who OD'd here,

        and, hours later—
at a boarded-up row house,
                    blackened windows,

        empty for years—
who was born here, and born again.
                    It's my house.

# 1989

I have heard of earth burial,
river burial, sky burial.
Being a poet I give you, Kirk
—though you are alive,
forgive me—an ink burial.
On a whim we hopped on my bike
and drove to California.
In a desert outside Montague
I ran out of gas.
We hadn't slept much.
Nobody in any direction.
One mountain far off
like a headless doll.
I felt I'd never seen
such a quiet road.
You were breakdancing.

## THE TERRIBLE BODY OF MY BULLY

I felt a sharp prick
in my side. There was Yanis,
after so many years,
and he'd stuck me
with a pen! Yanis
backed away through
the crowded bar,
with that same squinty look
as the old days, as if
aiming a dart at you.
It all came back.
He never looked you
in the eye. Even
as he held a brick
over your head
and dropped it hard
on your beautiful banana seat
bike, he looked away,
over your shoulder,
somewhere else. Yanis
later hanged himself
at his grandmother's house,
from a chandelier.
I knew that house.
I'd been friends
with his kid brother,
Red. Spent many
afternoons with Red
listening to Kiss records
and playing chess
under the chandelier.
After Yanis' death,

as his body decomposed
in the ground, his fists
crumbling like two old flags,
he was sighted often
at a sinkhole of a bar
in a polyester suit
sipping wine coolers,
hair greased as if awaiting trial
for armed robbery.
One night we are all
there—Mr. Mahoney
and his red whistle,
Kim and her volleyball,
Birdy and her bowl
of rock candy—
mingling like lunatics
in a Russian fable.
Some of us are tangoing.
Having a great time.
From the ceiling,
like piñatas, bodies
dangle. We keep dancing
five hundred years.
Pretending not to notice
their bare feet
in our hair.

## DRIVING TO THE AIRPORT WITH RAY

When I first got my license
I took my friend Ray for a drive.

He was the tallest guy
at our school.
And not beautiful.

Weak chin, big Roman nose,
red hair, blotchy skin.

And gay, which, in 1988
at Queen Elizabeth High,
made him a tough sell.

We chatted about
his roommate, who scared me.
Once, while she and I kissed

she pulled my hands
toward her breasts
as I pulled away.

Ray teased me,
"Don't you *like* breasts?"

We ended up at the airport
on a patch of grass
leaning back on our elbows.

I didn't feel the need
to entertain Ray.
He didn't act bored

or wonder aloud
why we were at the airport.

It was the year I started writing.
I told him a passing plane
looked *vivacious*.

I don't know
the details of Ray's death
but I see him alone

his high school traumas
seeping like an unbearable music.

"Do you even know,"
he said, grinning,
"what *vivacious* means?"

Grinning and shaking his head

his precious head
at my stupidity.

# THREE WEEKS OF HIGH SCHOOL FOOTBALL

I never liked football
but I admired the players
in our school halls,
their fratricidal affection:
murderous brothers,
wounded heroes
wrapped in tourniquets and flags,
barking Orphic songs.

I tried out, made the team.
First time I was tackled
I heard a crack
as if a croupier
had clapped his palms.
Earth the roulette wheel
spun, my soul
floated over the field
like pollen.

I quit the team.
Sat on my porch
reading every book in the house.
Life was good.

Now, thinking back,
I have that odd
lovely feeling
like something terrific happened
that I forgot.

The cosmos stretches out
from my porch.

A young girl walking her goat.
A blind man
with a psychopomp nose.
Sometimes it is the team
jogging by
singing the songs.

They arrive in the wind
and leave in the wind
like soap bubbles,
vanishing with a *pop*.
The very smallest sound.

# A Boy in the Process of Feeling Inexplicably Free

Four of us play cards
on Tampson's rug,
pretending to ignore June,
who I pine for,
and bucktooth Sean
under a blanket
slurping each other
like dogs. Days ago
that was me under the blanket
with June.

I'm *just* smart enough
to pretend to know
why notes are being passed
under the table,
why our cabals
have shifted, again.

On my walk home
I stop outside the red
brick gym of my school.
A big game inside.
Why don't I go in?
It doesn't matter.
It's springtime, dusk,
a big moon over
the empty schoolyard
and I am counting
cigarette butts, nudging them
with my sneaker.

My beautiful reader,
you've come this far with me.
I'd love to name for you
the very moment
I realized how happy
I can be.

The crowd in the gym erupts,
a sound that cascades
like confetti,
slow as a burning plane,
and I am a traveler
like those of the past,
resting on his way
across a badlands.

Or a dying moth
clinging to that traveler,
wings fluttering.
Any movement of the world
could blow it away.

## Portrait of June, Hand on Her Hip, Behind a Chainlink Fence

June chews gum
snapping her fingers
but there is no music.
Mr. Gallagher
our science teacher
slams his yardstick down,
June quivers. The phrase
is prophetic. Quivers
like a sparkler in the mind.
Walking home with June
it is autumn
we are horsing around
in the leaves,
I lower handfuls of red leaves
into her blouse
and gather them
out of the great nothing
the great everything
of her bra. My friends ask
if we neck,
I picture giraffes.
I am, at thirteen, fabulously
unprepared. You
may say, Okay
this is one dumb kid,
but still now
many years later
as I lean into a dream
there is June's face
smile crooked
messy black hair

in her eyes.
One evening we are kissing
I'm a little taller
I'm leaning back
on a neighbor's house
June pressed
in her striped shirt
against me
and it is raining.

## 1982

At the Puerta del Sol,
an armless mendicant
holds a plastic cup
in his teeth.
I drop a coin in it. *That sound—*

I'm twelve,
it is late, my parents
sleep, a quarter from my pocket
hits the floor.
Silence. Then
Dad's knees *crack*:
one, two. He nudges
my door open,
ducks under the chin-up bar.
He is naked,
he is hairy,
my orange Nerf hoop
a halo above him.
For one beat we both stare
ridiculously
at my Tarzan poster.
You are, he begins, fucking
careless, heartless ...
I listen.
In his swearing a silence—
in the silence
the fear he mixed
into my chocolate milk.
In the U.S. army,
Fort Bragg, N.C.,
Ansbach, Germany,

they woke him
in his bunk, barged
into his dream,
the drunks, the sergeants,
time and again.
There is an honesty
to our hysteria, his and mine,
and our division,
what we cannot speak
in daylight
naked between us.
He hesitates
before returning to bed.
I have said nothing,
fist clenched.
I had been masturbating.

## RESURRECTION FAIL

Strangers,
I like how our fingers brush
handing coins to and fro
at the market.
That communion.

On this spot
in the schoolyard
during recess
I walloped Bruce Church
in the gut.

I draw a slow smile
from the tough old bird
in a raincoat
at the bus stop.

I sit on a park bench
in new moon dark.
A crow in a black feather boa
in streetlight shadows
flirts with a dash of string.

Bruce, I'm sorry.
I was trying to impress a girl.
I have more rage
than I seem to.
I doubt my heart.

Love seems impossible, Bruce.
Though we exist
in its ripples.

Like the anatomy student
I once met
who slid the sheet
off a corpse
and there was
his childhood crush.

## Those Boys

I played two years, got one hit.
One hit *only*. Dad tried to help.

One hit. No friends of mine
on the team.

These were regal,
magisterial boys. Trotting bases,
nose-breathing. Prize horses.

I swear they did not sweat.

Once, alone in right field
I had to piss so bad
I closed my eyes
and saw the blood dancing.

I wanted them dead,
those boys,
I saw them dead, laid in boxes,

each clasping a bat
on his little pillow, cleats up.
Cut in their full beauty

like poisonous flowers.

# Centennial Pool

I climbed the ladder
to the high diving platform
near the ceiling,
looking down
like a cat on a branch—
the giant pool, the tiny people,
my father among them
beaming.

My young father in his swimsuit
proud as Tantalus
who stole nectar from Zeus
so his wife and children
could have a sip.

But that same Tantalus
sacrificed his kid:
cut his son Pelops to bits,
boiled him, served him
to the gods for lunch!

The gods chained Tantalus
to a fountain
with a killing thirst:
he bent down,
water bent away.

My father waves,
urging me to jump.

# 1980

I was not allowed to visit
Darren the bully
yet there I was
with Darren in his backyard
knee-deep in sheet metal
and car batteries.
"What a dump," I observed,
laughing. An idea skimmed
just under the water
of his face.

He kicked a car
hiked up on cinder blocks.
I kicked, too. It swayed,
heavily, and righted itself.

In his kitchen
a woman in a bathrobe
like molting feathers
smoked a cigarette.
We stepped past her.
"Is that," I snickered,
"your *mom*?"
Darren held his nose,
stuck out his tongue.

He adjusted the bunny ears
on the TV (Sergeant Schultz:
"I see *nothing!*").
We sat on the red shag rug.
"We have," I said,
"a better TV at my place."

He kept watching,
face pink and sweaty.

We watched TV a long time
without talking.
Finally I said,
"Your house sucks ass,
you know?" Darren
didn't look at me.
He was picking mac
and cheese out of a bowl
with his fingers.
Wheezing loudly.

## ONLY CHILD POEM

The self's hundred births converge
at daycare, awake at naptime
among the milk-fed sleepers.
Born apologizing for report cards,
born falling out of a school desk,
born exploding into a sprint
and *Jesus Christ Superstar* at recess.
O Guy Lafleur, where are you?
Born standing apart from the sleek
oracles of dodgeball, born wanting
Wally Martin's wolfboy grin.
Born loathing the weak ones,
the stupid ones. Born roller skating
from bullies. Spineless, bored,
euphoric, born dipping a big toe
in the shallow end of paranoia,
vandalism, stardust, dread.
Born hoarding *Tales of Suspense* #39.
Born confessing every secret
to Dad. Calm as an anthill,
tearing through a Citadel Hill
of Xmas gifts and out the back door
in a black eyepatch, *Ahoy!* Born
shooting Nerf baskets, fantasizing
that June's at the window
admiring me. Born in solitary,
back seat of a station wagon
traversing Maine, one-boy radio beacon,
frequency adjusted to guarantee
no witnesses. O Magic Johnson,
what leaks from a twenty centimeter
crack in the pit at reactor two?

Me at the dinner table, flicking
mashed potatoes at the scourge
of grade six, the first boy I kissed,
*Logan.*

# Saturday in Inwood, My Eighth Birthday, August, 1977

Aunts and aunts and aunts
In suffocating heat
And glass figurines
Dancing *en pointe*
On crocheted doilies

The face of my great-grandmother
Drifts toward me for a kiss
So slowly
Through the murk of balloons

My grandma in white pearls, flower print dress
And grandpa
In pressed slacks, golf shirt
Smile and laugh
With Sister Consolata, a nun

They, my grandparents, don't care for my dad
My awkward dad
Blowing smoke in their faces
Talking out of turn
Nibbling a green bean before grace is done

He wants to be part of the family
But not to change
To him they're strange
They don't speak plain
They speak in code, a fence he kicks
Like an unbroken horse

They don't care for his humor
His stories, his plans
They won't be charmed
This pains my mother
In her white pilgrim dress
Now squeezing my shoulder
Lightly

But I dig my dad
Catching my eye across rooms like these
Smiling his big smile
As if to say
*My boy we are above all these bastards*

Putting his forehead on mine
Making googly eyes
Kicking a football
Out in the street
High as he can

Here he is, the tall man
Bushy brown hair
Clapping for me as I blow out candles
On a chocolate cake

I'm leaning over it
As if to mash my face in it
But Dad
With two forefingers of his left hand
Urges my shoulder
Back
Which I understand

## Trained Bears

My fifth summer
between my long-haired parents,
rolling East in our blue
'64 Dodge truck,
California to Nova Scotia,
all we own out back
under flapping mackinaw blankets.
Truck a barge floating the earth
and we, Mister Man, are the Bargers.
For weeks on the highway
I am wind, the blue truck bone.
We roll to a stop in the woods.
At night beyond our wicklight,
the truck a dark mammal
in a larger darkness,
heavy among the singing frogs.
We carry an old brown horse
—eyes gaping, lips loose—
slow as the truck will go
along the dirt road.
In Halifax, Dad backs up
to my window. The blue truck
sleeps years in a coma,
going turquoise. Then, gone.
Gentle peasant, big hands,
dirt under the nails.
Silent big-boned uncle
with PTSD. When Dad
turned off the ignition

it shook for a few seconds.
I felt rather than saw
how it shook. I feel it still,

now thinking of how, years before,
Neal Cassady shook
after driving the Prankster Bus
all night on speed,
and his wife Carolyn held him.
Gabbing too fast, too much,
amok. Sight gags, tricks.
He gallops, prances, dances,
story-tells, pill-pops,
driving, driving, driving!
His anachronistic parlance—
kundalini, state troopers,
Armageddon, John 15:1
—paranoic riffing without climax,
whirlpools of words
turning, turning
as if by their own power.
You were the Beat
who could not write.
Skinny, tense, smile a tripwire.
Fallen gnomic prophet
out of a Blake poem,
pestilential monk
out of *The Canterbury Tales*,
whose monologues
charm us for a few pages.
Sweet, social, obedient.
A trained bear, Carolyn
called him. One day in '68,
in Guanajuato, Mexico,

Cassady, in T-shirt and jeans,
blind drunk, staggered
into a wedding party,
drank wine, ate tortillas
and secobarbital. Later
crawled on hands and knees
out into the rain. At forty-one,
past tired, his body quit.
On that railroad track
they laid a tarp upon him.

# THE TRIUMPHS OF 1974

Broke, we move to California.
Riverside, mall-land.
Dad scores a government job:
computer programmer,
missile systems. Rusted rockets
aiming at your head
as you walk in. He hates it.
Buys a new Triumph motorcycle.
Parks it in our living room.
Drives us three on it
to my nursery school: my mom
on back, me on the tank.
I'm hyper. Others nap
while I watch. A nurse says,
Give the kid stability.
Another, Ritalin. Fuck that,
says Dad, Let's move
to Canada. Thin again,
antsy. Sick of Nixon,
Vietnam. The day he quits
we dance in the kitchen,
arms flying. He drives me
to the dirt hills of a nearby lot.
Hour of train whistles,
smoggy sky
hallucinatory red.
That sense of your father's joy.
Almost too much joy,
him behind you, singing,
*Almost cut my hair*
*It happened just the other day*
*It's gettin' kiiiinda long.*
I hold the great metal tank.

# 1969

In a 19th century brick infirmary
on Staten Island
my gory face crowns,
I cough and spit,
a beached sea-beast.
On the other coast
Manson's *family*
is smearing "Death To Pigs"
on the walls of Leno
and Rosemary LaBianca
in blood. My father points to me
through the glass.
Women are burned alive
in Qui Nhơn, Vietnam;
my mother surfaces
from anesthetic; Nixon
hosts salmon dinner;
moon astronauts wave
in a ticker tape hurricane;
Brezhnev hurls a bust
of Stalin at his TV.
My father drives us home
in a Ford Fairlane.
Yankees up 10-3 in the 7th.
At Woodstock
Hendrix improvises
a star-spangled howitzer reverie.
Bundled in serapes,
I bawl for a breast.

# THE DELIGHT OF MISAPPREHENSION

Ever hear, far off, a grinding,
some big machine in the wrong gear—
then realize with a pang
it's an animal in pain?
Once I heard a hawk scree,
opened my door to find
a kitten, a stray, gazing at me, eyes cold.
It's hard to hear right.
Just ask the Arizonan mother
resting her head on the chest of a girl,
not resting, *listening*
to her son's heart, transplanted
into this tiny brown chest.
In antique times those who died abruptly
they called gods. Since that's not
an Arizonan custom,
the dead boy (still just
a boy) leans his ear
on a splintered wall,
listening to the dogs fighting
just beyond it.
Which is a woman
breathing.

## PATRILINEALITY

I glide among the dead
males of my line
Irishmen and Norwegians
bristling comically
clearing their throats
with a horrible authority
scalps reeking of
whiskey and hair tonic.
O magnificos!
Did I mention they're naked?
O starvelings
in this dusty ballroom,
erections trembling
like stamens in
some deathless garden
of the *Rig Veda*.
Is that the far-off sound
of an army marching?
No, it's their wrinkled fingers
rapping the tables,
heavy rings stamped
with old world marks.
I'd like one of them
to notice me, my cigars,
my motorcycles.
I went to a bullfight!
(And left in tears.) How much
I'd love to chew the fat
with this Bud Abbott
look-alike, about firetrucks
or *Anna Karenina*,
but he is sticking a gun

into his mouth.
No, a whiskey bottle.
I sit beside an unspecified
great-great-great-
great-grandfather
stonejawed
in a Confederate hat.
He lights a handrolled cigarette.
Then suddenly I am
my own mother
in a striped miniskirt
in English class
feet on the next desk
and he is my dad
smoking, eyeing me.
Within me
a palpable kick.

# Acknowledgments

My thanks to the editors of publications in which the following poems first appeared:

*32 Poems:* "The Delight of Misapprehension"; *American Poetry Review:* "Resurrection Fail" (I); *Antioch Review:* "Patrilineality"; *ARC Poetry Magazine:* "Swimming in Church Lake, Nova Scotia"; *The Awl:* "Resurrection Fail" (II); *Beltway Poetry Quarterly:* "Saturday in Inwood ... " and "1980"; *Cimarron Review:* "1982"; *The Dalhousie Review:* "Morning after a Party in a Farmhouse"; *E-Verse Radio:* "Those Boys"; *failbetter:* "I Received a Bitter Email ... "; *Freefall:* "1989"; *Grain:* "2014"; *The Hopkins Review:* "When I Heard My Childhood Name Cried Out" and "Dog Songs"; *Literary Matters:* "The Handsomest Man in the Neighborhood," "Rais Bhuiyan Song," "I Saw Two Beat Poets ... ," and "Trained Bears"; *Malahat Review:* "A Big Black Wave"; *ONE ART:* "How to Float"; *Philadelphia Stories:* "The Epic of Senge"; *Plume:* "The Triumphs of 1974"; *POOL:* "Only Child Poem"; *The Puritan:* "Resurrection Fail" (IV); *Skylight 47:* "Portrait of June ... "; *THINK:* "2016"; *The Winnipeg Review:* "Resurrection Fail" (IV).

Deep abiding gratefulness to Indran Amirthanayagam, Fayyaz Vellani, Warren Longmire, Luke Bartolomeo, Ernie Hilbert, Luke Stromberg, Vasiliki Katsarou, Daniel Jones, Savannah Cooper-Ramsey, Patrick Blagrave, Cameron MacKenzie, Tim Fitts, Steven Kleinman, Anthony Rivel, Kyle Brown-Watson, Paul Siegell, Matthew Wong, Sun Man Ho, Blair Reeve, Stephanie Bolster, Micheline Maylor, Kate Rogers, Brian Bartlett, Tonja Gunvaldsen Klaassen, Jim Johnstone, Aimée Parent Dunn, Stephanie Yorke, Jami Macarty, James Arthur, Ryan Wilson, Vijay Seshadri, Eduardo C. Corral, David Yezzi, Jean Barger, Tiina Rosenqvist, for the love and friendship and, when I was lucky, late night porch wine.

To Erin Belieu, whose keen critical eye and long-distance phone calls helped so much in mooring this book to the dock.

To Monita Wong for her kind permission to use her son Matthew's painting, *End of the Day*, for the cover.

To the judges of the 2020 Grayson Books Poetry Contest for choosing *Resurrection Fail* as a finalist.

To The Hambidge Center, where I made significant progress on these poems while I was artist in residence.

To the Canada Council for the Arts for assistance during crucial stages in the development of this book.

To Spuyten Duyvil Press for making cool books.

JOHN WALL BARGER is the author of four books of poetry: *Pain-proof Men* (2009); *Hummingbird* (2012), finalist for the Raymond Souster Award; *The Book of Festus* (2015), finalist for the J.M. Abraham Award; and *The Mean Game* (2019), finalist for The Phillip H. McMath Book Award. He is a contract editor for Frontenac House, and teaches in the BFA Program for Creative Writing at The University of the Arts in Philadelphia.